Greetings from Los Angeles

Pd $5 at Phoenix Bks, SLO   27 July 1989

LA-118- Carthay Circle Theatre, Los Angeles, California

1B-H1019

Greetings from Los Angeles

A Visit to the City of Angels in Postcards

Kerry Tucker

Steam Press ★ Cambridge, Massachusetts

DISTRIBUTED BY KAMPMANN & COMPANY

Published, 1982, in the United States by Steam Press, Inc.,
16 Walden Street, Cambridge, Massachusetts 02140

Distributed by Kampmann & Company, 9 East 40th Street,
New York, New York 10016

Designed by Hal Morgan
Composition by DEKR, Woburn, Massachusetts
Printed and bound in Hong Kong.

ISBN: 0-942820-00-2
LC: 82-50690

Introduction

WELCOME TO LOS ANGELES—a shimmering, sprawling metropolis as celestial as its name suggests—where palm trees sway like South Sea dancers against the skyline, where a single vista can contain both snow-capped mountains and golden orange groves, and where the world's most sophisticated system of freeways whirs and ticks with all the precision and complexity of a fine Swiss watch. It is a city built on contradictions and dreams by ingenious entrepreneurs, where fabulous tar pits full of prehistoric fossils coexist quite happily with sumptuous department stores, where movie theaters masquerade as Chinese shrines and Egyptian palaces, where starlets are discovered in drugstores, and where a day at the beach is a distinct probability.

Untold millions of visitors have been drawn to this city of marvels—to the dazzle of Hollywood, and to the chance to eat in a restaurant shaped like a hat, buy bread in a windmill bakery, gaze through glass-bottomed boats off Catalina, or listen to an orchestra play under the stars. The sights are endless and the climate is sublime.

And any sight that a visitor to Los Angeles has ever seen has been captured forever in the form of the picture postcard. As strange, wonderful, and infinitely varied as the city itself, these small pictures form a priceless record of changing Los Angeles. They show the ever-undulating skyline of the city, the amusements on the old Venice midway, and the fabulously ornamented ceiling in the lobby of the once-magnificent Alexandria Hotel and form a pictorial record unparalleled in its scope and detail.

The earliest cards—printed during the first two decades of this century—document a time when the city was dominated by its downtown, and when the tourist trade first found Los Angeles. The lavishly produced cards from this era—many printed in ten or more colors—show Pershing Square at its peak, the long-gone amusements on Mount Lowe, and that once famed but now forgotten tourist sight—the ostrich farm. Later the rise of Hollywood was recorded by the intensely colored, boldly airbrushed linen postcards introduced in the late twenties, often embellished by the printer's retoucher with dramatic cloud formations, searing

sunsets, and beautifully lurid rays of light. These cards seem especially appropriate for conveying the allure of the homes of the stars: a small circular portrait of the resident often floats in a corner of the card, or the star is shown relaxing—out of context—in the foreground. The glossily laminated four-color postcards that have dominated the market since the 1950s just as appropriately convey the sleekness of the city's post-height-limit skyscrapers, glass-and-steel structures, and ever-growing freeways.

Although many publishers have produced postcards of Los Angeles, the Western Publishing and Novelty Company surpasses all others in the breadth and beauty of its postcard views of the city. Founded in 1910, the company has published spectacular cards in almost every available finish. Western's linen cards, printed by the Curteich Company of Chicago, are almost unearthly in their beauty; the views are composed with fastidious care and drenched with luminous colors that lift them light years beyond the realm of most postcards. Other companies that have produced fine postcard views of Los Angeles include the Newman Post Card Company of Los Angeles, whose cards of the city at the turn of the century are delicately colored and finely detailed, and the M. Kashower Company, whose early "homes of the stars" cards are highly prized by collectors today.

The postcards on the following pages will take you to several

Los Angeleses—the historian's Los Angeles, the tourist's Los Angeles, the architect's Los Angeles, the movie lover's Los Angeles, and, most of all, the dreamer's Los Angeles.

Welcome to the City of Angels. There's no other place like it in the world.

Greetings from Los Angeles

THE OLD PLAZA CHURCH/CHURCH OF OUR LADY THE QUEEN OF THE ANGELS

535 North Main Street
José Antonio Ramirez, master builder. 1822

At the center of the oldest part of Los Angeles, the Old Plaza Church has been in continuous use since its dedication on December 8, 1822. Built with proceeds from the sale of brandy and cattle donated by friars of the San Gabriel Mission and parishioners, the original structure was simple; its adobe walls, tar-covered roof, timber rafters, and pounded-earth floor were crafted with the help of local Indians employing native materials.

The church's first bell was a gift from the San Gabriel Mission. Another, known as the "elopement bell," was given by Captain Henry Fitch as penance for having whisked the lovely Josefa Carrillo off to Chile, where the couple wed without her parents' consent. When they returned to California the following year with an infant son, Fitch was arrested on charges of abduction and imprisoned at the San Gabriel Mission. He was later freed, but with the order to redeem himself by giving a bell to the church in the plaza. Fitch's penance hangs alone in the southwest wall of the bell tower (not visible in this view), which was once a gazebo-like structure, but was later remodelled into a squat campanile. Two other bells, gifts from the San Gabriel Mission in 1827, hang in the front of the tower along with the first.

The Old Plaza Church has weathered several sieges of remodeling, but retains much of its early pueblo spirit.

Old Plaza Church, Los Angeles, Cal.

13

LA-30—Main Entrance, Union Station, Los Angeles, California

9A-H916

UNION PASSENGER STATION

800 North Alameda Street
John Parkinson, Donald B. Parkinson, J. H.
Christie, H. L. Gilman, and R. J. Wirth,
architects. 1939

In 1933 the Santa Fe, Union Pacific, and Southern Pacific railroads joined forces to build the Union Passenger Station, an $11-million mission moderne marvel constructed on the site of what used to be the city's Chinatown. By May 7, 1939, the station was ready for the public eye, and more than 1.5 million visitors toured the new facility during its three-day dedication ceremonies, which featured an epic pageant called the "Romance of the Rails."

The front of the building, which is truncated in this view, stretches 850 feet along Alameda Street and is crowned by a 135-foot-high observation tower. In its prime the station used thirty-nine sets of tracks, which, along with the building and ramps, sprawled over forty-eight acres. Among the station's attractions were two profusely planted patios and the elegant Fred Harvey's restaurant and bar, garnished with eighteenth-century Spanish provincial appointments.

LA-29—Waiting Room, Union Station, Los Angeles, California

9A-H918

The central waiting room, which offered travelers the latest in comfort and beauty, featured acoustical tile, indirect lighting, and enormous upholstered leather chairs. Much of what is shown in the view above remains intact; a row of the chairs has been reupholstered with vinyl, but the seemingly endless strip of mosaic tile that runs the length of the room and the timber-look rafters have stayed just as they were when the station opened.

Today Union Station sees only a fraction of the crowds it once served, but the building remains one of the world's most beautiful tributes to railroad travel.

15

Court House, Los Angeles, Cal.

LOS ANGELES COUNTY COURTHOUSE

Spring and Temple Streets
Built 1891. Demolished 1936

The cornerstone of this imposing building was laid on April 26, 1888, and the courts moved in and opened for business on August 10, 1891. The city spent $500,000, which included the cost of an elevator, on the red sandstone structure. Later an outdoor windowed elevator was installed in one of the building's niches. Dubbed the "honeymoon tower" because couples ascended it to the marriage license office, it soon became one of the city's favorite tourist attractions.

The courthouse suffered severe damage in the earthquake of March 10, 1933, and was afterward declared unsafe for occupancy. Workers hired to demolish the building opened the cornerstone and found a two-cent stamp, a medical prescription signed by a Dr. Kurtz, a copy of the Los Angeles *Times*, and a county letterhead.

The Los Angeles Criminal Courts Building occupies the corner now.

CITY HALL

Southwest corner of Temple and Main
Streets
John C. Austin, John Parkinson, and Albert
C. Martin, architects. 1928

For more than a generation the 454-foot-high
Los Angeles City Hall reigned as the city's
tallest building—a soaring and spectacular ex-
ception to the city's 150-foot height restric-
tion, lifted in 1959.

Even more imposing than the building's
height is the speed with which it was constructed. The cornerstone—its mortar mixed
with water from twenty-one California missions—was laid on June 26, 1927, and the
building was dedicated the following April.

All facades to the third floor are of California granite, and the tower and the two five-
story wings are faced with matte-glazed terracotta.

The beams of light shown radiating from
the apex of the tower in this view come from
the Colonel Charles A. Lindbergh Beacon.

LA·170   LOS ANGELES CITY HALL

121857

17

THE LOS ANGELES TIMES BUILDING

First Street and Broadway
Built 1886. Destroyed 1910

A four-page edition of Harrison Gray Otis's Los Angeles *Times* on October 1, 1910, announced the catastrophe: "Unionist Bombs Wreck the Times; Many Seriously Injured." Although local unionists at first placed the blame for the explosion—which killed twenty people and destroyed the three-story building—on faulty gas fixtures, union organizers Joe and Jim McNamara, defended by Clarence Darrow, confessed to having masterminded the bombing. Jim was sentenced to life imprisonment, and Joe, who had not been directly involved with the crime, was sentenced to fifteen years.

The message on the back of this card, dated October 3, 1910, reads: "This the Times Bld. was recked and 20 men lie buried in the ruines . . . slow work so hot the Brick."

6A-H17

THE LOS ANGELES TIMES BUILDING

202 West First Street
Gordon B. Kaufmann, architect. 1935

This mammoth building now houses the Los Angeles *Times*, which was founded in 1881 and has been owned by the same family since 1882, when Harrison Gray Otis became its publisher and editor.

Built of beige limestone and ornamented with bronze grillwork, the present building contains the corporate of- fices of the Times Mirror Company as well as twelve newspaper presses capable of printing up to sixty thou- sand copies of the *Times* every hour. A neck-stretching mural by Hugo Ballin, called *Newspaper*, lines the ro- tunda.

An annex, the Times Building South, was constructed in 1948, and in 1974 William Pereira and Associates ex- tended the headquarters with a sleek bronzed steel and glass wing.

19

See photo, p. 43. Ford Times, Dec 1946!

Angel's Flight, Los Angeles, Cal.

ANGEL'S FLIGHT

Third and Hill Streets
Colonel J. W. Eddy, engineer. 1901.
Removed 1969

For more than six decades, people too weary to mount the precipitous stairway to the summit of Bunker Hill could ascend instead on what was billed as the world's shortest incorporated railway—Angel's Flight. Two counterbalanced cable cars, "Olivet" and "Sinai," each capable of carrying thirty-two passengers for the fifty-second trip, traveled the celestial incline.

In 1905 the flight was regraded to a uniform thirty-three degrees, and the white cars shown here were replaced by black and orange ones. The simple arch at the base of the incline was replaced in 1908 by a far more elaborate white marble one, and the following year, when the Elks held their national convention at their new temple near the top of the flight, the letters "B.P.O.E." were added to the top of the arch.

Los Angeles, Cal.

The hundred-foot-tall observation tower Colonel Eddy constructed at the crest of the hill afforded a dazzling view of the city, which during the first quarter of the century resembled the one shown above. The tower near the center of the picture belonged to what until 1928 was Los Angeles's City Hall. The rooftop an inch to the tower's right, crowned by a tent shape, is the Bradbury Building; the tent shape is its enormous skylight. The observation tower was torn down in 1938, and tall buildings soon obscured the angel's view of the city.

In 1969 the much-loved railway was dismantled and stored to make way for redevelopment of the Bunker Hill area, which included planing of the hill. Although the Community Redevelopment Agency, responsible for the project, promised to reinstall Angel's Flight within two years, the pieces remain locked away in a warehouse.

1528-30

THE RICHFIELD BUILDING

555 South Flower Street
Morgan, Walls, and Clements, architects. 1929.
Demolished 1970

This beautifully proportioned skyscraper, gleaming with a black-glazed terracotta surface overglazed with pulverized gold particles, was for years the most striking office building in downtown Los Angeles. Its exterior colors were a direct reference to the company's "black gold" product, as was the oil-derrick-style sign tower.

Four highly stylized symbolic figures by sculptor Haig Patigian stood watch over the main entrance: "Aviation," a female carrying an airplane propellor; "Postal Service"; "Industry"; and "Navigation," and the building swarmed inside and out with art deco details.

The eighty-foot-tall sign tower was destroyed by fire in December 1967, and the water used to douse the flames damaged much of the rest of the building. In 1970 the once-stunning Richfield Building was razed to make way for the Atlantic Richfield Tower. Two of the original building's twenty-foot-high sculpted bronze doors stand like tombstones at the rear of the new building.

RICHFIELD BUILDING, LOS ANGELES, CALIFORNIA   T 136

The Richfield Bldg, 1926-1968
  by David Gebhard,
a 27 page book of text & pix.
in slip case, is at Cal Poly Library
3rd floor, filed as
XX/NA/735/L55/G44
            also
an article fd in
Calif. Arts & Architecture mag.
  some date in 1930.
  filed in same area in library

146 EDISON BUILDING, LOS ANGELES

1A1343

THE EDISON BUILDING/ONE BUNKER HILL BUILDING

601 West Fifth Street
Allison & Allison, architects. 1931

When the thirteen-story general office building of the Southern California Edison Company was finished in 1931, it glowed inside and out with the latest in electrical developments, including a revolutionary new air-cooling system that could be reversed and used to heat the building during cold weather. The building also boasted an elaborate system of pneumatic tubes, for whisking messages from office to office, and drinking water treated with ozone. Murals devoted to "Power," "Transmission," "Distribution," and "White Coal" were commissioned for the lobby walls.

After four decades, Edison outgrew the building and moved to other quarters in 1971. Since then the building has been owned by the One Bunker Hill Company, and much of it is occupied by the First Business Bank.

THE LOS ANGELES PUBLIC LIBRARY

650 West Fifth Street
Bertram G. Goodhue, architect. 1926

The stunning Los Angeles Public Library stands on the site of what was once the State Normal School. The building was Bertram Goodhue's last major work, and it looks very much like a compressed version of his Nebraska State Capitol.

The Flower Street facade shown here was the most elaborate of the building's original entrances, and, during the library's early years, the lawn before it featured a three-tiered pool punctuated by "The Well of the Scribes." A carved panel over the doorway depicts a torch race, and two sculpted figures—Phosphor and Hesper, the Heralds of Light—stand sentinel above it. Unfortunately, most of the library's oasis-like landscaping has been converted into parking lots.

The library's holdings are extensive, and its California Collection is world renowned. With its sixty-one branch libraries it serves thousands of readers every day.

25

Dr. J. Whitcomb Brougher

The Auditorium, Home of the Temple Baptist Church, Los Angeles, Cal.

Dr. Robert J. Burdette

PHILHARMONIC AUDITORIUM/TEMPLE BAPTIST CHURCH

427 West Fifth Street
Charles F. Whittlesey, architect. 1906

Looming over Pershing Square from the northeast, the mammoth home of the Temple Baptist Church replaced an entertainment center called Hazard's Pavilion, which for two decades had provided Los Angeles with cultural events, including performances by Sarah Bernhardt, Nellie Melba, and Mark Twain.

In 1905 a syndicate made up of Mrs. Robert Burdette and friends bought Hazard's, razed it, and, with the Temple Baptist Church, built what they billed as the largest combination auditorium, office, and church in the world. In addition to Dr. Burdette's sermons, visitors to the 2,700-seat auditorium could attend operas, movies (*Birth of a Nation* premiered there), and, from 1920 until 1964, concerts by the Los Angeles Philharmonic.

In 1938 the building received an alarming facelift, which replaced the Gothic ornamentation shown here with a moderne shell.

THE BILTMORE HOTEL

515 South Olive Street
Schultze and Weaver, architects. 1923

When the Biltmore first opened its Spanish Renaissance doors in October 1923, the management celebrated by inviting a galaxy of stars—among them Theda Bara, Myrna Loy, Ramon Navarro, and Mary Astor—to admire the furnishings and to dine. Possibly the most memorable item on the evening's menu was the hotel's hostess, Peggy Hamilton. Dressed in a white satin gown decorated with replicas of the paintings by Giovanni Smeraldi that graced the hotel ballroom, she was carried on a platform through the attentive crowds.

The thousand-room hotel—at the time the largest west of Chicago—soon became devastatingly fashionable, and in 1928 the owners added a five-hundred-room extension to accommodate the expanding guest list.

The owners who renovated the Biltmore in 1976 cleaned and restored Smeraldi's murals and did much to rekindle the glitter and elegance of the hotel's early days.

27

Marble Lobby, Hotel Alexandria, Los Angeles, Cal.

THE ALEXANDRIA HOTEL

210 West Fifth Street
John Parkinson, architect. 1906

In its prime the Alexandria shimmered with sumptuous appointments and film stars. One reporter announced that going into its lobby was like "walking into New York City." Guests' feet all but disappeared in the cloud of Turkish carpets (Tom Mix later scandalized the city by riding his horse on them); ten enormous marble pillars touched the twenty-eight-foot-high ceiling; and the main banquet room, which later became known as the "Palm Court," was lit by a 196-square-foot stained-glass skylight.

The hotel fell on hard times in the early thirties, and in 1934 closed its doors. An unambitious new owner allowed the hotel to decline even further, and by the 1950s it was the seedy haunt of boxers and their fans; the ballroom served as a training ring.

A new owner restored much of the Alexandria in 1970, but the lobby as it appears here is gone forever.

Songs You'll Love

Clifton's "Pacific Seas"
618 So. Olive St., Los Angeles

CLIFTON'S PACIFIC SOUTH SEAS CAFETERIA

618 South Olive Street. 1931. Demolished 1960

Clifford E. Clinton opened his first cafeteria with the policy, "Pay what you wish. Dine free unless delighted" in 1931, and discovered after three months of business that he'd served more than ten thousand free dinners. Undaunted, he opened a nearby "Penny Kitchen," where a modest meal could be had for small change, and put prices on the food in his main cafeteria.

A trip to Hawaii inspired Clinton and his wife, Nelda, to recreate the South Seas for their patrons, and soon a waterfall spilled over the entrance, and the interior bloomed with tropical plants made from neon, grass huts, and exotic murals. Inspired by their tropical success, the Clintons opened Clifton's Brookdale Cafeteria on South Broadway and decorated it like a redwood forest where diners could eat from their trays while tucked into grottoes rimmed by babbling brooks.

Clifton's Pacific South Seas was demolished in 1960, but the Brookdale still offers good food in unusual surroundings at a reasonable price.

THE BRADBURY BUILDING

304 South Broadway
George H. Wyman, architect. 1893

The first impression the Bradbury Building conveys is of an office building turned inside out. In the center of a huge skylit open court twin birdcage elevators operate with all their mechanisms exposed; ornately detailed cast-iron staircases and galleries line the space like outsize ribs. Everyone who isn't in an office with the door closed can see everyone else, and the entire court is drenched with light.

The Bradbury Building is an architectural wonder, and a large part of the wonder is that it was the first building designed by George H. Wyman, a man who never had any formal training as an architect. Wyman was an unknown draftsman when mining mogul Louis Bradbury asked him to design an office building. Bewildered, Wyman sought the advice of his dead brother, who spoke to him through a Ouija board. "Take the Bradbury Building," said the brother. "It will make you famous." Wyman did, and his brother's prediction was fulfilled.

A devotee of Edward Bellamy's utopian novel *Looking Backward*, Wyman had been impressed by a description in that book of a typical office building of the year 2000. It would be "a vast hall full of light, received not alone from the windows on all sides but from the dome. . . ." Wyman designed the Bradbury to fulfill his futuristic fantasies, and the result was a building that looks otherworldly even today.

Restoration in 1969 saved the Bradbury from decay—it had been converted into garment factories in the 1940s—and the building is now home to law offices, an advertising agency, and the regional headquarters of the American Institute of Architects.

PART OF THE VESTIBULO OF THE BEAUTIFUL BRADBURY BUILDING, LOS ANGELES, CAL.

BROADWAY AT NINTH, LOS ANGELES

THE EASTERN COLUMBIA BUILDING

849 South Broadway
Claude Beelman, architect. 1930

Adolph Sieroty, owner of two chains of retail stores, the Eastern Outfitting Company and the Columbia Outfitting Company, built this $2-million cerulean blue and gold-leaf shaft to house the general headquarters of both concerns. An Eastern store, which sold furniture, and a Columbia store, which sold clothing, originally occupied the first four floors of the building, and the rest of the Eastern Columbia's thirteen floors housed offices and employee conveniences, including an auditorium, tea and lunch rooms, a library, and a roof garden.

To allow room for a parking garage beneath the building, architect Beelman concealed the heating, lighting, and air-purifying apparatus in the building's magnificent clock tower, and to preserve the sleek exterior he tucked the fire escapes inside corner tunnels.

Today the Eastern Columbia is one of the most outstanding examples of art deco architecture in Los Angeles, and, appropriately enough, is the home of the Los Angeles Conservancy, a society devoted to the preservation of the city's landmarks.

THE COCA COLA BOTTLING COMPANY BUILDING

1334 South Central Avenue
Robert V. Derrah, architect. 1937

When Stanley Barbee, president of the Coca-Cola Bottling Company of Los Angeles, commissioned Robert Derrah to update the company's three buildings in 1937, Derrah responded by encasing them in an ocean-liner-like shell, complete with portholes, metal railings, and a ship's bridge—all probably as much a reference to Barbee's love of the sea as to the cleanliness and soundness of Coca-Cola's bottling methods. The sleek and stylish result is Los Angeles's supreme example of marine moderne design.

The building, which is ornamented with outsize terracotta Coca-Cola bottles, was restored to its original nautical radiance in 1976.

115423

THE AUTOMOBILE CLUB OF SOUTHERN CALIFORNIA

2601 South Figueroa Street
Hunt and Burns, architects. 1923

By crusading for the construction and maintenance of good roads, the Automobile Club of Southern California—"Friend to all motorists since 1900"—can claim its share of credit for the development of Los Angeles's suburbs and freeways and for the decentralization of Southern California. By 1922 the club, which had been founded in the office of a member, boasted seventy-five thousand members and a nearly completed headquarters at the corner of Adams and Figueroa. The building had doubled in size by 1931.

The club started its ambitious sign-posting effort in 1905, and in 1909 began publishing *Touring Topics* magazine—now known as *Westways*—which reports monthly on California history and culture.

THE NEW HOME OF THE
LOS ANGELES
EXAMINER

J. MARTYN HAENKE ARCHITECT
ASSOCIATED WITH
MISS JULIA MORGAN :

Built of re-inforced concrete; Spanish Colonial type; 323 feet long, 110 feet deep.
The Examiner has a greater circulation than any of its contemporaries; on Sunday
a greater circulation than that of all the other Los Angeles Sunday papers combined.

THE HERALD EXAMINER BUILDING

1111 South Broadway
Julia Morgan, J. Martin Haenke, and W. J. Dodd, architects. 1912

Julia Morgan, the first woman trained at the Ecole des Beaux-Arts in Paris, received a number of architectural commissions from the Hearst family, including the ones for San Simeon, the Bavarian village at Wyntoon, and the Herald Examiner Building—originally the Examiner Building. Inspired by the California Building at the 1893 Chicago World's Fair, Morgan designed a gleaming bar of mission revival white and orange to house William Randolph Hearst's newspaper enterprise. She created private quarters for Hearst in the domed tower, which offered a panoramic view of the city.

Hearst later acquired the *Herald* and the *Express* and merged the two in 1931. In 1962 that paper combined with the *Examiner* to form the present *Herald-Examiner*, still headquartered on South Broadway.

35

LA-155   Al Malaikah Temple, Shrine Auditorium, Los Angeles, California

BA-H114

AL MALAIKAH TEMPLE/ SHRINE AUDITORIUM

3228 Royal Street
G. Albert Lansburgh, architect. 1925

Described as "neo-penal Baghdad" by Los Angeles *Times* writer Martin Bernheimer, Shrine Auditorium rose in 1925 from the ashes of the Shriners' first Los Angeles auditorium, which had burned down in 1920. The new 6,700-seat structure was at the time of its dedication the largest indoor auditorium in the world. Its stage, a cavernous 186 feet wide and 72 feet deep, has been the scene of a variety of entertainments, including "The Miracle," a 1927 spectacular for which the entire auditorium was converted into a Gothic cathedral, seven years of Academy Award presentations, performances by Rudolf Nureyev and Maria Callas, and countless circuses.

106. Coliseum, Exposition Park, Los Angeles, Calif.

LOS ANGELES MEMORIAL COLISEUM

3911 South Figueroa Street
John and Donald Parkinson, architects. 1923. Enlarged 1931

This grand stadium stands on a site once used for horse, greyhound, and camel racing. In 1910 citizens rallied against the low life in the area, tore down the race track and the bars, and began improvements on what is now Exposition Park.

Construction of the coliseum began in 1921, on a prom-

ise from a trustee of U.S.C. that the university's football team would play its home games there. To save excavation money, the stadium was designed to fit in an old gravel pit. The coliseum was enlarged in 1931 to accommodate the Olympic Games, held in Los Angeles in 1932, and in 1958 a baseball stadium was constructed inside the arena to house the newly Angelized Dodgers, who won the World Series there the following year. The coliseum is now home to the U.S.C. and U.C.L.A. football teams. Its largest crowd, of 134,254, came to hear Billy Graham on September 8, 1963.

37

WATTS TOWERS/THE TOWERS OF SIMON RODIA

1765 East 107th Street, Watts
Built by Simon Rodia from 1921 until 1954

In 1921, equipped with a window washer's belt and bucket, tile setter's tools, and apparently unlimited patience, energy, and imagination, Simon Rodia set to work on what would eventually become one of the most fabulous structures ever built by one man. For the next three decades Rodia's towers, three large and four small, climbed skyward over his Watts neighborhood like otherworldly beanstalks. He built their skeletons from steel rods and wire-reinforced cement, then covered them with seashells, pieces of broken bottles and dishes (one tower is studded almost entirely with glass from Seven-up bottles), and bits of wood. Rodia rimmed the base of the towers with fountains, birdbaths, a gazebo, and a model of a ship and enclosed the entire mosaic garden with an elaborately decorated wall. He strung the towers—the tallest is over a hundred feet high—with electric lights and allowed neighbors to use the fountains for baptisms. Rodia told some neighbors that the towers were a memorial to his wife. Others heard that they were a tribute to Christopher Columbus and that the three tallest represented the *Niña*, the *Pinta*, and the *Santa Maria*. Rumor had it that he'd buried his wife beneath them, that he'd buried his car beneath them, and that the tallest was Tokyo Rose's radio tower.

Rodia deeded his lot to a neighbor and left Watts abruptly in 1954. His house, which had adjoined the towers, burned down in 1955. By 1959 the entire lot was in ruins, the city had declared the towers a safety hazard, and they were scheduled for demolition.

That year two advocates of Rodia's work, William Cartwright and Nicholas King, with help from the Los Angeles County Museum of Art, established the Committee for Simon Rodia's Towers in Watts, and waged a dramatic battle to save the structures. Their efforts culminated in a pull test designed by a missile-test engineer to prove that the towers were strong and safe. The towers withstood ten-thousand pounds of pressure, revealing Rodia as an engineering genius as well as a master craftsman.

Rodia died in Martinez, California, in 1965, aware that his life's work had been spared. The Department of Cultural Affairs of Los Angeles now maintains the towers, and the Watts Towers Art Center has been built nearby.

Watts Towers

Tournament of Roses, New Year's Day, Pasadena, Cal.

PASADENA TOURNAMENT OF ROSES PARADE

Every New Year's Day since 1890 wondrous floral extravaganzas have floated through the streets of Pasadena, a soothing sight for many a bloodshot eye. From gaily decorated carriages and buggies in the early years, entries have blossomed into massive displays of mechanical wizardry, each still covered entirely with fresh flowers and greenery.

The accompanying East-West football game—the Rose Bowl—began tentatively in 1902, when the University of Michigan played Stanford and beat them 49 to 0. Chariot races filled in until 1916, when the Brown University football team was persuaded to make the trip west to meet Washington State. East-West games have capped Pasadena's New Year's festivities every year since.

The Busch Garden (the finest sunken Garden in the world), Pasadena, Cal.

BUSCH GARDENS

Thirty acres on both sides of Arroyo Boulevard between Bellefontaine Street and Madeline Drive
Robert G. Fraser, landscape architect. 1903. Converted into homesites 1937 and 1944

Not to be confused with the Busch Gardens amusement park, the elaborately landscaped Busch Gardens in Pasadena were commissioned in 1903 as a private project by Adolphus Busch, then president of Anheuser-Busch.

Busch spent $2 million to landscape his incredible back-yard, which contained fourteen miles of pathways, moss-rimmed pools, terraced hills, thousands of plants and shrubs, an old mill, and clay figures of fairy-tale characters. Between 1921 and her death in 1928 Busch's widow kept the gardens open to the public, donating the proceeds to war veterans. The gardens also served a stint as Sherwood Forest to Erroll Flynn's *Robin Hood*.

Half the gardens were subdivided in 1937 and the rest in 1944. Portions of them may be found in Pasadena backyards today.

13365 RIDING AN OSTRICH, CAWSTON OSTRICH FARM, SO. PASADENA, CAL.

THE CAWSTON OSTRICH FARM

South Pasadena
Founded by Edwin Cawston, 1883. Closed 1934

Edwin Cawston imported his first shipment of ostriches from South Africa in 1883 and soon built a brisk business from their feathers, which were in heavy demand for collars, cuffs, muffs, hats, and fans. Soon ostrich farms were springing up all over California and for the next thirty years flourished both as an industry and as tourist attractions.

Visitors to the Cawston Farm could watch the plucking process, have their pictures taken on a stuffed bird, or feed the ostriches oranges for the thrill of watching the bulge go down the birds' throats. Many of Cawston's ostriches had names, among them General and Mrs. Grant, Admiral Dewey, and Mr. and Mrs. McKinley.

Some say that the feathers, which tore off easily in the wind, lost favor with the fashionable when the automobile grew popular. Whatever the cause, the industry collapsed during World War I, and most of the farms disappeared. The Cawston Farm held on as a tourist attraction until 1934.

CHRISTMAS TREE LANE

Santa Rosa Avenue from Woodbury Road
north to Foothill Boulevard
Planted in 1882

This majestic, mile-long double row of Deodar cedars was planted a century ago along both sides of what was then the driveway to the Pasadena home of John Woodbury. The millionaire was so smitten by the trees while on a trip to India that he sent for seeds of his own. The cedars now stand over eighty feet tall and measure sixty feet around.

In December 1920 Fred C. Nash, founder of the Christmas Tree Lane Association, strung the trees with electric lights, sparking a Christmas tradition that has dazzled thousands of viewers ever since, with interruptions only during World War II and the energy crisis of 1973.

43

MOUNT LOWE

At the northern edge of Pasadena

In 1891 Professor Thaddeus C. Lowe, inventor, scientist, and balloonist, organized the Pasadena and Mt. Wilson Railway Company, popularly known as the Mt. Lowe Railway, and began to build a three-thousand-foot cable incline from Altadena to the top of Echo Mountain. The railway opened on July 4, 1893, when a brass band ascended the incline playing "Nearer my God to Thee."

Lowe's railway, like Angel's Flight on Bunker Hill, used two counterbalanced cars on parallel tracks. One ascended while the other descended, and each balanced the load of the other. Its cars, named "Rubio" and "Echo," took passengers to the three-story Chalet, one of two hotels in the Lowe complex; to a menagerie; to a post office where souvenir postcards were postmarked "Mount Lowe," and to the terminal for an electric trolley. The trolley took passengers on a winding track deeper into the mountains, which included a thrilling spin across the precariously perched circular bridge shown here and on to Crystal Springs and Ye Alpine Tavern, where guests could take in a meal and the view or stay overnight in an Alpine bungalow.

CIRCULAR BRIDGE, ELEVATION 4200 FEET, MT. LOWE, CALIFORNIA.

Largest Searchlight in the World on Echo Mount, Calif.

Visitors to Lowe's complex could also inspect Inspiration Point, where Lowe installed a three-million-candle-power searchlight that had been featured at the 1893 Chicago World's Fair. The lens, which without its metal cover weighed eight hundred pounds, projected a beam of light so powerful that a newspaper held in its path thirty-five miles away could be read at night; the beacon was visible for a hundred fifty miles over the ocean.

Reflected upside down in the lens in the view above is Echo Mountain House, the largest of Lowe's hotels. It

HOUSE-KEEPING COTTAGES, YE ALPINE TAVERN, MT. LOWE, CALIFORNIA.

burned to the ground in 1900, and five years later the Chalet and menagerie burned, too. The incline itself fell to fire in 1935, followed two years later by the Alpine Tavern. The great rain and floods of 1938 finished off Lowe's creation, and in the 1950s the ruins were razed.

Today the only signs that the celestial city ever existed at all are traces of building foundations and gears, ties, and rails that once helped guide Professor Lowe's twin chariots up the mountain.

San Fernando Mission, California.

THE SAN FERNANDO MISSION

15151 San Fernando Mission Boulevard

The San Fernando Mission, seventeenth in the chain of twenty-one California missions, was founded on September 8, 1797, and for the next three decades prospered as a model mission. The friars and the Indians together built a sophisticated irrigation system; gardens, vineyards, and orchards flourished; and mission buildings contained a tannery, smokehouse, carpentry and blacksmith shops, and facilities for the manufacture of soap, candles, and olive oil.

The Mexican government secularized the California missions in 1834, and soon the San Fernando Mission fell into disrepair. During the Mexican-American War the property was sold for a rancho, which became known as the "Ex-Mission San Fernando." It was returned to the Catholic Church after California became a state.

Restoration began in 1898 and continued periodically until 1948, when the mission was fully repaired.

Motor Car at the S. P. Depot San Fernando, Cal.

RAILROADS IN LOS ANGELES

In 1868 Phineas Banning persuaded the City of Los Angeles to build its first railroad, connecting the downtown business community with the deep-water anchorages at Wilmington/San Pedro. A decade later, in exchange for control of the Wilmington line, the Southern Pacific Railroad agreed to include the city in its route from San Francisco to Yuma, a development that profoundly affected the city's growth. Eventually the Southern Pacific's lines radiated in five directions from downtown Los Angeles—first to San Fernando, then to San Bernardino, Anaheim, Wilmington, and Santa Monica—charting the course of the city's future growth.

In 1885 the Santa Fe entered the city, triggering fierce rate wars between the two great railroads, and in 1905 the Union Pacific established itself as the city's third major line.

FOREST LAWN MEMORIAL PARK

1712 South Glendale Avenue
Dr. Hubert L. Eaton, founder; Frederick A. Hansen,
landscape architect. 1917

When Dr. Hubert Eaton planned Forest Lawn, he expressed a desire that it become "a great park, devoid of misshapen monuments . . . where lovers new and old shall love to stroll." The Glendale cemetary is now world renowned for both its tenants and its trappings. Jean Harlow, W. C. Fields, Tom Mix, and Marie Dressler are among those who repose there, and Forest Lawn's collection of sculpture and paintings is remarkable. The Memorial Court of Honor, which Eaton planned as a "New World Westminster Abbey," contains a mammoth stained-glass re-creation of "The Last Supper," as well as the tombs of seven "immortals"—including Carrie Jacobs-Bond, the composer of "I Love You Truly"; Gutzon Borglum, who carved Mt. Rushmore; and Dr. Eaton himself.

In "The Mystery of Life" sculpture shown opposite, eighteen figures—including "the learned philosopher scratching his head in vain" and "the sweet girl graduate lost in dreams"—contemplate a pair of courting birds. The stone court that surrounds the group is inscribed with the lyrics to Victor Herbert's song "Ah, Sweet Mystery of Life."

7A-H3617

51

THE ANGELUS TEMPLE

1100 Glendale Boulevard
Brooke Hawkins, builder and contractor, from designs by Aimee Semple
McPherson. 1923

Soon after Aimee Semple McPherson's arrival in Los Angeles in 1918, the imposing figure in white satin robes had eclipsed every other evangelist in the city. Her sermons were spectacular blends of rhetoric containing biblical and movie references—one compared Jesus Christ to the Lone Ranger—and they brought her followers by the thousands. By 1921 McPherson's Church of the Foursquare Gospel had the funds to begin the construction of a mammoth permanent headquarters overlooking Echo Park.

The 5,300-seat Angelus Temple, which McPherson dedicated on New Year's Day, 1923, is designed like a Broadway theater, with rows of tiered seats dropping down to the orchestra pit—where a young Anthony Quinn once played trumpet in the Temple's band—and to the stage, where Mc-Pherson held forth from a red-velvet-cushioned chair.

In 1924 McPherson began to broadcast "The Sunshine Hour" every morning over station KFSG—"Kalling Foursquare Gospel"—and in 1925 she constructed the Lighthouse of Foursquare Evangelism, or L.I.F.E. Bible College, adjacent to the temple, for the training of ministers and missionaries.

McPherson's luminous career was dimmed occasionally by scandal, most dramatically when she disappeared into the surf at Venice Beach in May 1926, only to surface a month later in Arizona with a feeble story about having been kidnapped. Although the press tore her story to shreds—a fair amount of evidence indicated that she had faked drowning in order to run off with a male friend—she remained steadfast to her account and many in her congregation believed her.

McPherson died in 1944, leaving her ministry in the care of her son Rolf, who in 1972 refurbished and restored much of the Angelus Temple.

650:—The Angelus Temple, Los Angeles, Calif.

3081 — Palm Walk, Echo Park, Los Angeles, California

ECHO PARK

Glendale Boulevard and Park Avenue

In 1868 a dam twenty feet high was erected in the area now known as Echo Park, creating a lake that allowed farmers in the area to operate a grist mill. Twenty-two years later the lake and adjoining property were given to the city as a public park, and in 1899 the English landscape architect Joseph Henry Tomlinson was hired to plan the flora and its layout. Tomlinson modeled the park on a garden in Derbyshire and trimmed its twenty-six acres with a lotus pond, a wide variety of semitropical plants, and hundreds of palm trees.

The Echo Playground, built in 1907 at the south end of the lake, is the oldest playground in Los Angeles.

Westlake Park Scene in Winter, Los Angeles, Cal.

WESTLAKE PARK/MACARTHUR PARK
Wilshire Boulevard between Alvarado and Park View

In 1886 the City of Los Angeles received a desolate thirty-two-acre mudhole from George Smith and George S. Patton as part of a land exchange. The next year a resourceful Mayor William Workman secured five hundred dollars from Los Angeles residents, which he matched with city funds to build a public park. The swamp was filled with topsoil, pepper trees were planted, and the dismal little pond was enlarged into a ten-acre lake rimmed with a forty-foot-wide drive.

By 1890 Westlake Park was a major tourist attraction, and visitors came in droves to hear Sunday concerts at the bandstand and to row on the lake.

Wilshire Boulevard now bisects the park, which was rechristened in 1942 in honor of General Douglas MacArthur.

WILSHIRE BOULEVARD

Sixteen miles from downtown Los Angeles to the Pacific Ocean in Santa Monica

H. Gaylord Wilshire, banker, millionaire, socialist, and developer of the I-on-a-co electric cure-all belt, subdivided what he called the Wilshire Tract in 1885. It included the land between Sixth and Seventh streets from Parkview to Benton Way and an unpaved road through the center, which Wilshire named for himself.

Today the celebrated boulevard traverses several widely varying Los Angeles neighborhoods. The area from Harbor Freeway to Lafayette Park contains new immigrants from Southeast Asia, Mexico, the Philippines, and Central America; while from Lafayette Park to La Brea Avenue the boulevard is lined with professional firms. The section from La Brea to La Cienega, dubbed the "Miracle Mile" by promoter A. W. Ross in the thirties, is still a shopper's paradise.

BULLOCK'S WILSHIRE

3050 Wilshire Boulevard
John Parkinson and Donald Parkinson,
architects. 1929

"Like a jewel of jade upon the breast of a Titian goddess, Bullock's Wilshire gleams against the California sky," reported smitten Olive Gray, covering the opening of the department store for the Los Angeles *Times*. The still-dazzling Bullock's Wilshire represented a radical step in the history of Los Angeles department stores: it was located away from the then-fashionable downtown shopping district, it featured a separate entrance designed for motorists, and it was absolutely the last word in moderne decorations.

When the store opened, it featured a "Doggery," which offered the latest in canine fashions; a "Collegienne" department; an octagonal shoe salon; and a "Desert Lounge," decorated with the colors of the desert, real cactuses, and a glass ceiling painted with a desert landscape by Herman Sachs, who also painted the history of transportation mural on the motor court ceiling.

Raymond Chandler immortalized the store in a pivotal scene in *The Big Sleep*: Philip Marlowe recalled that "the violet light at the top of Bullock's green-tinged tower was far above us, serene and withdrawn from the dark, dripping city" when he bought information from Agnes Lozelle at the east entrance to the parking lot.

TYPICAL WINDMILL BAKERY STORE

VAN DE KAMP'S HOLLAND DUTCH BAKERS/STORE NO. 1

Corner of Western Avenue and Beverly
Boulevard
H. G. Oliver, designer. 1921

In 1915 brothers-in-law Lawrence L. Frank and Theodore Van de Kamp opened a potato chip stand with a Dutch-door service counter on South Spring Street. Soon they added macaroons and pretzels to their line and business boomed. In 1921 a Van de Kamp windmill bakery sprouted at the corner of Western Avenue and Beverly Boulevard. It was the first of eighty such structures, which soon became Los Angeles landmarks. Because of them, a generation of Los Angeles children believed that bread came from windmills.

The prototype Van de Kamp windmill was designed by Henry Oliver, who later became a well-known Hollywood set designer. The blades really did turn in the wind, and the salesclerks wore Dutch costumes. All the stores were prefabricated at a central construction site in three parts—blades, base, and tower—and moved to their locations by flatbed truck. If the location wasn't profitable, the windmill was simply snapped apart and reassembled at another site.

The rise of the supermarket in the thirties forced Van de Kamp's to locate inside grocery stores, and the individual windmills slowly faded from the Los Angeles landscape. The company, which continues to flourish, now punctuates its signs with a Delft-blue neon windmill.

THE BROWN DERBY

3377 Wilshire Boulevard
Built 1926

This dapper dome was the idea of Herbert K. Somborn and playwright Wilson Mizner, who, according to legend, decided one evening that anyone who knew anything about food could "sell it out of a hat."

In its early years the Brown Derby on Wilshire was a favorite haunt of Hollywood celebrities, including Somborn's wife, Gloria Swanson, who brought her own vegetarian meals from home, Clark Gable, Carole Lombard and of guests from the Ambassador Hotel across the street. Soon three other Brown Derby restaurants opened in the Los Angeles area, but only the original had the shape of a hat.

In September 1980 the restaurant's owners suddenly laid off their employees, closed the doors, and began to pry the bowler apart. Alarmed friends of the Brown Derby waged a quick and effective battle for its preservation. Today the hat remains securely on its original site, and will be incorporated into a new development in 1982.

59

In the Valley at Hollywood, Cal.

HOLLYWOOD

What is now the film capital of the world started out as a sleepy rural community in the Cahuenga Valley. During the boom real-estate year of 1887, 640 acres in the valley were subdivided. Horace Henderson Wilcox bought 120 of them, divided his purchase into lots, and offered them for sale as "Hollywood," a name chosen by his wife in honor of the summer home of a friend near Chicago.

Hollywood grew slowly and sedately at first, and in 1903 the community's five hundred residents incorporated as a city, with local regulations that included the prohibition of poolrooms and liquor stores.

The tranquil community was sent spinning by the arrival of the first movie studio in 1910, and the next year residents agreed to be annexed to the City of Los Angeles.

An Outdoor "Set" built in-doors, Christie Studios, Hollywood.

CHRISTIE STUDIOS

Northeast corner of Sunset Boulevard and Gower Street

In September 1910 David Horsley and Al Christie moved their fledgling Nestor Film Company from Staten Island to a former tavern on the corner of Sunset and Gower in Hollywood. Although a number of other picture makers, including D. W. Griffith, had already been lured west by the promise of year-round sunshine, Nestor was the first film company to locate in Hollywood. By January 1911 fourteen others had established themselves there, and Hollywood's reputation as the land of motion pictures was secure.

Universal acquired the Nestor site in 1912, and the following year the studio burned to the ground. Universal soon rebuilt and expanded the structure, then moved to North Hollywood, once again leaving the studio in the hands of Al Christie, who for many years produced the Christie Comedies there with his brother Charles.

61

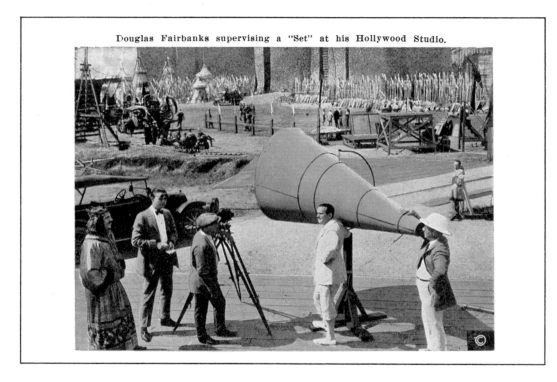

Douglas Fairbanks supervising a "Set" at his Hollywood Studio.

SET FOR THE MOVIE *ROBIN HOOD*

Santa Monica Boulevard and Formosa

For most of 1922 the fabulous sets for the Douglas Fairbanks production of *Robin Hood* ranked as one of Los Angeles's biggest tourist attractions. Its centerpiece, a replica of Nottingham Castle, towering ninety feet over a stretch of Santa Monica Boulevard in West Hollywood, was rimmed by a real moat, and its drawbridge could be raised and lowered with the aid of concealed motors.

In this view, Wallace Beery, who played Richard the Lionhearted in the picture; Robert Florey; Arthur Edeson; Douglas Fairbanks; and Alan Dwan, who designed the castle, wait for the shooting of the tournament scene to begin. The trucks in the background support wind machines, which will set the pennants flying.

Charles Chaplin Studio, Hollywood, Los Angeles, California.

THE CHAPLIN STUDIO/A & M RECORD STUDIO

1416 North La Brea Avenue at Sunset Boulevard
Built 1918

Charlie Chaplin built this Tudor-style studio complex in Hollywood in 1918, and, although the building has changed hands many times since then, it still looks almost exactly as it did the day it opened.

Chaplin filmed many of his finest pictures here, including *The Gold Rush*, *The Kid*, *The Circus*, *City Lights*, *The Great Dictator*, and *Modern Times*. He also left his footprints in cement in front of one of the sound stages.

The studio was later owned by Red Skelton, who sold it to CBS in 1962, who subsequently sold it to A & M Records, the present owners.

778:—Hollywood Hotel, Hollywood, Cal.

THE HOLLYWOOD HOTEL

Hollywood Boulevard between Highland and Orchid
Built 1902; subsequently enlarged. Demolished 1956

When Almira Parker Hershey first saw the Hollywood
Hotel it was a small, elegant, stucco structure nestled in
the quiet town of Hollywood—just the sort of hotel to
capture the heart of a chocolate heiress. She bought it,
added a lobby, chapel, ballroom, and garden, and in-
creased the number of guest rooms just in time to accommodate the stream of movie people who poured into the
neighborhood in 1911. Miss Hershey's hotel soon catered
to a galaxy of early picture stars, including Rudolph Val-
entino, Jean Acker, Norma Shearer, and Nazimova. The
names of celebrities who attended the hotel's dances reg-
ularly were painted in gold stars on the ballroom ceiling.

The Hollywood Hotel was later overshadowed by more
luxurious hotels. It fell into disrepair in the forties and
was razed in 1956.

HOLLYWOODLAND

IN THE HILLS OF HOLLYWOOD, CALIFORNIA

643-29

HOLLYWOODLAND

North of Franklin Avenue, between Western Avenue and Vine Street, to the top of the Santa Monica Range Tracy E. Shoults, Co., developer. 1923

In 1923 a group of influential Angelenos—Harry Chandler, General M. H. Sherman, E. P. Clark, S. H. Woodruff, and Tracy Shoults—formed a syndicate to reap the rewards of the real-estate boom in Hollywood. They subdivided the old Sherman and Clark ranch in the hills above the movie capital, put in picturesque winding roads, and promoted the lots with a vengeance.

The mountainside land that others had avoided as being difficult to build on was touted by the syndicate as the healthiest place to live in all Los Angeles. "The kiddies that are raised in the hills have husky limbs and lusty lungs. . . . You will find in Hollywoodland the Dream Place of your visions." The sign for the development, visible at the top right of this card, was certainly a stroke of genius. Minus its last syllable, it has become a modern landmark.

THE HOLLYWOOD SIGN

Near the summit of Mount Lee
John D. Roche, designer, 1923. Replaced 1978

The magnificent Hollywood Sign sprawls 450 feet across the face of Mount Lee. The brainchild of a twenty-six-year-old advertising man, it was originally erected to promote Hollywoodland, the subdivision at the top of Beachwood Canyon in Hollywood. The original letters, each fifty feet tall, were built on sheet-metal panels attached to a framework of pipe, wire, scaffolding, and telephone poles, and went up at a cost of $21,000. For a decade and a half the gargantuan "Hollywoodland" blazed from the hillside, outlined at night by thousands of electric lights and kept in pristine condition by its caretaker, Albert Kothe, who lived in a cabin behind one of the "L"s. Its only dim moment was the 1932 suicide of aspiring starlet Peg Entwhistle from the top of the "H."

In 1939 maintenance was discontinued. Souvenir seekers wrenched all the lightbulbs from their sockets, and panels blew off in the wind. Six years later the development company gave the neglected sign and adjoining acres to the City Recreation and Parks Department, and in 1949 the Hollywood Chamber of Commerce repaired the surface, but not the lights, of the first nine letters and razed the last syllable, leaving "Hollywood." The restoration was short-lived, however; by the 1960s the sign was derelict once more. Hollywood Kiwanis members patched it up in 1970, but what the sign needed was stable, long-term care.

A massive campaign launched by rock star Alice Cooper in 1978 finally produced the funds to dismantle the old sign and replace it with a sturdier, weatherproof one. The new sign was unveiled on November 11, 1978, and has gleamed staunchly ever since.

World Famous Hollywood Sign

877--Easter Sunrise Services, Hollywood Bowl, Hollywood, California

7B-H2074

THE HOLLYWOOD BOWL

Entrance, 2301 North Highland Avenue
First stage, 1921; enlarged, 1926; first shell, Lloyd
Wright, architect, 1927; second shell, Lloyd Wright,
architect, 1928; present shell, Allied Architects, 1929

In 1919, spurred by the rapid growth of their community,
residents of Hollywood began a search for a place to stage
outdoor cultural events. After much roaming of the hills
and singing to the bushes, they settled on Daisy Dell—

now the Hollywood Bowl.

The first Easter sunrise service was held in 1922, and
the same year Alfred Hertz conducted the first of the
famous "Symphonies Under the Stars" concerts. In 1926
the bowl's overseers touched up the shape of the natural
amphitheater, installed seats, and commissioned Lloyd
Wright—Frank Lloyd Wright's son—to design an acoustic
shell.

Wright's shell was thriftily built with discarded lumber
from Douglas Fairbanks's *Robin Hood* set, but its shape

861—Entrance to Hollywood Bowl, Hollywood, California

OB-H2581

looked too much like an Indian tepee to survive the critical eye of the Hollywood cognoscenti. Wright's second attempt, erected the following year, was of a more conventional design, but it met with disaster when it was left unprotected in the winter rains. The present shell, designed by a group of local architects, is made of welded airplane steel and can be moved on rollers built into its base.

The sculpture at the Highland Avenue entrance to the bowl was carved by George Stanley and erected in 1940 with the help of the Works Progress Administration. In a sleek, streamline moderne style, its three figures represent music, drama, and dance.

Over the years the Hollywood Bowl has been the scene of many of the greatest events in music, from performances by Lily Pons and Margot Fonteyn to the Beatles and Frank Sinatra. It continues to provide one of the most spectacular concert settings in the world.

GRAUMAN'S EGYPTIAN THEATRE

6708 Hollywood Boulevard
Meyer and Holler, architects. 1922

Sid Grauman's remarkable Egyptian Theatre, the first big movie house in Hollywood, would have delighted the eye of Ramses himself. Grauman, who built his theaters according to the principle that waiting for a movie must be at least as exciting as the movie itself, lined the narrow entrance to the Egyptian with small import shops, painted the walls with Egyptian-style motifs, and hired an actor to dress as a Bedouin and walk back and forth atmospherically along the flat roof.

Inside the Egyptian theme was carried out in compulsive detail. Each side of the stage was flanked by two enormous columns and a sphinx, and a night scene of a ruined temple beside the Nile was painted on an asbestos scrim. Even the ventilating system was given the pharaonic treatment: the sixty-foot air-intake valve was designed to look like Cleopatra's Needle. The 1,700-seat theater opened on October 18, 1922, with the world premiere of Douglas Fairbanks's *Robin Hood*; a gala event at which Cecil B. DeMille presented Grauman with a laurel wreath on behalf of the movie colony.

The Egyptian has undergone several radical facelifts since Grauman sold it in 1927. The shops are gone; two new theaters have been added; the large columns to the right in this view have been removed; and a very un-Egyptian marquee now obscures the entrance portal.

825. ENTRANCE TO GRAUMAN'S EGYPTIAN THEATRE, HOLLYWOOD, CALIFORNIA.

93362

774:—GRAUMAN'S CHINESE THEATRE, HOLLYWOOD, CALIF.

The girl ushers, wear wonderful Chinese costumes & etc.

GRAUMAN'S CHINESE THEATRE/MANN'S CHINESE THEATRE

6925 Hollywood Boulevard
Meyer and Holler, architects. 1927

Having whetted moviegoers' appetites for the exotic with his Egyptian Theatre, in 1927 Sid Grauman offered even headier fare. The sumptuous Chinese Theatre opened on May 18 of that year with the world premiere of Cecil B. DeMille's *King of Kings*. Guests at the opening passed through a forecourt planted with cocoa palms, received their tickets at a box office dressed as a garden pagoda, filed past a pair of massive white marble Chinese Heaven Dogs, and watched the movie in a shrinelike auditorium dominated by a colossal chandelier modeled on a Chinese lantern.

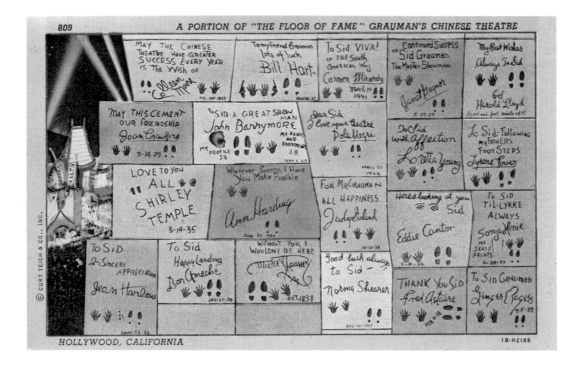

HOLLYWOOD, CALIFORNIA

The "Floor of Fame," which now covers much of the theater's forecourt, owes its origin to Norma Talmadge, who, when touring the theater shortly before it opened, with Mary Pickford, Douglas Fairbanks, and Sid Grauman, accidentally stepped in a patch of wet cement. Grauman asked Pickford and Fairbanks to do the same, and today the forecourt crawls with the foot- and handprints of more than 160 stars. There are even a few flourishes:

Sonja Henie immortalized her skate blades, Betty Grable printed her leg, and Al Jolson left a kneeprint.

A new owner fitted two new theaters into the complex in 1979 and rechristened it "Mann's Chinese Theater" in honor of himself, but for devotees of the Chinese palace it will always be Grauman's.

CAPITOL RECORDS TOWER

1750 Vine Street
Welton Becket, architect. 1954

Rising thirteen stories above the intersection of Hollywood and Vine, the Capitol Records Tower looks for all the world like a stack of monstrous records. According to one story, the idea for the shape came from Nat "King" Cole and Capitol's president Johnny Mercer. But the official line is that the round design was chosen for reasons of efficiency.

The rectangular blocks at the base of the tower house three recording studios. Each rests on a sound-insulating layer of asphalt-impregnated cork. Frank Sinatra was the first to use the recording studios when, in February 1956, he conducted a fifty-six-piece orchestra.

At the top of the trylon spire above the building, a red beacon continuously spells out "Hollywood" in International Morse Code.

8A-H3107

NBC RADIO CITY

Northeast corner of Sunset Boulevard and Vine Street
O. B. Hanson, architect, with the Austin Co. 1938.
Demolished 1964

An elegant example of streamline design, NBC Radio City was a building of the future that, ironically, succumbed to rapid advances in technology.

The smooth, blue-green exterior was broken by banks of glass brick that seemed to invite the outside in. The main lobby, in the corner section, opened to the full three-story height of the building, and the entire wall facing the main entrance was covered by a heroic mural depicting the "genie of radio." NBC's master control room was visible from the lobby through a large window.

After NBC moved into television in the forties, Radio City was quickly outmoded. In 1964 the building was torn down, and a bank now stands on its site.

75

"CROSS ROADS OF THE WORLD"
HOLLYWOOD, CALIF.

CROSSROADS OF THE WORLD

Front entrance, 6671 Sunset Boulevard
Robert V. Derrah, architect. 1936

Like a cruise ship docked in downtown Hollywood, with souvenirs of its world travels scattered around it, Crossroads of the World is a remarkable apparition. The central ocean-liner building is outfitted with portholes and a sun deck and crowned in the fore by a tower with a spinning eight-foot globe. The other buildings in the complex represent the world and are built in a kaleidoscope of architectural styles—Spanish, French, Italian, Mexican, Moorish, Turkish, Medieval English, Cape Cod, and Early American.

The Crossroads was originally opened as a shopping center—an early mall—but has since given way to offices. Happily, the present tenants keep the complex shipshape, and visitors will still be dazzled by its extravagance.

872—The Original Farmers Market, Hollywood, California

PHOTO BY "DICK" WHITTINGTON   1B-HZ152

FARMERS MARKET

6333 West Third Street
Roger Dahlhjelm, Fred Beck, and Earl Gilmore, developers. 1934

In 1933 Roger Dahlhjelm approached Earl Gilmore with the idea of setting up a farmers' market in his field at Third and Fairfax in Hollywood. With the help of Fred Beck, Dahlhjelm drove around the San Fernando Valley and talked seventeen farmers into delivering truckloads of produce. Business was slow at first, but when Hedda Hopper and Gail Patrick talked the market up among their movie star friends, the crowds started to pour in. Visitors hung around for hours hoping to see Joan Crawford or Clark Gable buy tangerines.

Today Farmers Market is one of Los Angeles's foremost attractions. Over forty thousand people browse through its stalls on an average day, choosing from a cornucopia of temptations—exotic fruits, pastries, cheeses, and cafe-style meals from around the world.

77

THE CARTHAY CIRCLE THEATER

6316 West San Vicente Boulevard
Dwight Gibbs, architect, 1926. Demolished 1969

The Carthay Circle Theater, Los Angeles's only movie theater with a pioneer motif, opened on May 18, 1926, with the world premiere of Cecil B. DeMille's *The Volga Boatman*.

The frontier spirit affected the Carthay inside and out: the promenade held two fountains—one dedicated to the memory of the pioneer mother, the other crowned with a statue of a man panning for gold—and the inside, which was designed as a nearly perfect circle, contained an eleven-section mural devoted to pioneer history, photographs of the Old West, and a study of the Donner Party painted on the curtain.

The Hollywood premiere of *Gone With the Wind* took place at the Carthay on December 27, 1939, as iridescent an opening night as Hollywood has ever seen. Searchlights lined the streets for two blocks on both sides of San Vicente Boulevard, producing a blaze of color visible for miles, and ten thousand spectators jammed the area around the theater, desperate for a glimpse of Clark Gable or Vivien Leigh. When minutes before curtain time, fifty seats in the center of the theater remained empty, David O. Selznick, who had reserved them for his own party and then forgotten about them, sent aids scrambling to nearby homes to invite fifty bewildered neighbors of the Carthay Circle to be Selznick's guests at the gala—the last and most glamorous movie event of the decade.

Gone With the Wind returned to the Carthay Circle screen once more, in 1968, and played there for almost a year. Soon after the run finished, the venerable theater was demolished to make way for an office building.

159 CARTHAY CIRCLE THEATRE, LOS ANGELES, CALIFORNIA

123733

1A-H392

BEVERLY HILLS ELECTRIC FOUNTAIN

Intersection of Wilshire and Santa Monica Boulevards
Ralph Flewelling, architect. 1931

In 1931 the City of Beverly Hills acquired and beautified a park along the north side of Santa Monica Boulevard in order to shield the lavish residential section to the north from the business section to the south. The electric fountain, at the Wilshire Boulevard end of the park, caused nightly traffic jams when it was first unveiled, and city planners wondered whether they would have to dim the colored lights in the interest of safety. Changing water spouts and lights from twenty-eight floodlamps produced sixty different effects every eight minutes. Fortunately, motorists got used to the fountain, and its plays of light and water were allowed to continue.

A kneeling figure of an Indian praying for rain graces the top of the central pedestal, and a frieze around the base, by artist Merrel Gage, depicts the history of California.

80

L.A.33. BEVERLY HILLS HOTEL AND BUNGALOWS. BEVERLY HILLS, CALIF.

61516

BEVERLY HILLS HOTEL

9641 West Sunset Boulevard
Elmer Grey, architect. 1912

Sprawling over twelve acres, with 315 rooms and twenty-one bungalows, the Beverly Hills Hotel is the Rolls Royce of Los Angeles-area hotels—the place to be seen with stars and producers.

Paul Newman, Ingrid Bergman, Henry Kissinger, Paul McCartney, and the late Shah of Iran have all stayed there, and Elizabeth Taylor practically grew up there—her father ran an art gallery in the lobby. Howard Hughes kept a cluster of bungalows for twenty-five years—at a cost of $250,000 a year—until he moved to Las Vegas in 1967.

The Polo Lounge, which occupies the former children's dining room, is the place where much of the movie industry's big business is conducted. Joan Didion dubbed it "the home of the Deal." Erlichman, Haldeman, and Mitchell were eating lunch there, in booth two, when the call came through that the Watergate scandal had broken.

81

PICKFAIR

1141 Summit Drive
Hunting lodge remodeled into a home by Wallace Neff, 1919

When Douglas Fairbanks bought this lodge high in the Beverly Hills the area was a wilderness, howling with coyotes, which had dissuaded the fainter hearted from even considering living there. But when Fairbanks and Mary Pickford took up residence in their lavish aerie after their marriage in 1920, the rest of the movie colony followed suit, studding the hills with palatial homes, of which Pickfair is still the crown jewel.

The Fairbankses spared no expense in outfitting their home; they installed one of the earliest private projection systems and a two-hundred-foot-long swimming pool with a sand beach, built a replica of a frontier saloon to serve as a recreation room and to hold Fairbanks's collection of cowboy chaps, and at one time maintained a series of man-made ponds for canoeing.

For years an invitation to Pickfair was tantamount to a command performance. Pavlova danced there, Maurice Chevalier sang there, Calvin Coolidge lunched there, and in 1922 Lord and Lady Mountbatten made the guest wing their honeymoon cottage.

The Fairbankses divorced in 1936, and Mary Pickford lived at Pickfair with Buddy Rogers, her second husband, until she died in 1977. Sports mogul Jerry Buss bought the estate in 1980 for $5.3 million, roughly a hundred fifty times what Fairbanks paid for it in 1919.

793:—HOME OF MARY AND DOUGLAS FAIRBANKS, BEVERLY HILLS, CALIF.

867 THE HOME OF JACKIE COOGAN, LOS ANGELES, CALIFORNIA

OFF FOR THE STUDIO

HOME OF JACKIE COOGAN

Oxford Street at Wilshire Boulevard

Jackie Coogan leapt into the hearts of moviegoers with his role alongside Charlie Chaplin in *The Kid*, released in 1920. The following year he starred in *Peck's Bad Boy* and *Oliver Twist* and established himself as the most famous self-made rich kid in America.

The author Gene Stratton Porter, a neighbor on Oxford Street, remembers that Jackie woke up every morning by sliding down a chute from his second-story bedroom into his swimming pool—and that he woke the neighbors with his shriek upon hitting the water.

In 1922 the Coogans moved into a new home on Crescent Heights Boulevard. The old house was torn down in the course of Wilshire Boulevard's dynamic growth.

713 BUNGALOW DRESSING ROOM OF SHIRLEY TEMPLE.

20TH CENTURY-FOX FILM STUDIOS

HOME OF SHIRLEY TEMPLE
20th Century-Fox Film Studios

Shirley Temple launched her movie career at age four, in *The Red-Haired Alibi*, but it was not until she reached the riper age of six that she became a real star, with the success of *Little Miss Marker*. In the same year—1934—she acted in eight other movies, and 20th Century-Fox built her a private bungalow on their lot in order to keep her on hand. Childsize in every detail, her home away from home was furnished with tiny chairs and a sofa covered in chintz "of an intriguing kindergarten design."

When not working, Shirley lived with her parents in Santa Monica. There she had a pale blue and peach bedroom, a color scheme not complemented by her doll, teddy bear, and stuffed lamb.

85

HOME OF MARION DAVIES

Pacific Coast Highway, Santa Monica
Built in stages, 1926 to 1930. Main house dismantled
1956

In 1926 William Randolph Hearst built Marion Davies a
modest $7,500 beach home. Over the next few years he
added to it in a grandiose way, with massive doses of gold
leaf, specially commissioned carvings, and entire rooms
imported from Europe.

When finished, the cottage had 118 rooms, fifty-five
baths, and sixteen telephone lines. Tudor-style paneling,
antique murals, and priceless mantel pieces were all assembled in the "Hollywood-historical" interior. The 1740
bedroom of the Earl of Essex in Hertfordshire was
shipped from England and reassembled as a projection
room. Two swimming pools graced the grounds, the one
on the ocean side spanned by a marble Venetian bridge.

Eventually Davies grew tired of the house and sold it.
The main house was torn down in 1956, and today the
guest house and other parts of the estate serve as a private
beach club.

303:—Marion Davies and Her Colonial Beach Home, Santa Monica, Calif.

PORT LOS ANGELES, CAL.
"THE LONGEST WHARF IN THE WORLD."

LONG WHARF AT SANTA MONICA

Thompson Bridge Co., engineers. 1893. Dismantled 1921

During the 1880s the dramatic growth of Los Angeles made it apparent that an adequate deep-water shipping port was needed. No natural harbor existed, and various factions argued the merits of competing plans. In 1892 the Southern Pacific Railroad took matters into its own hands and began work on a 4,700-foot-long wharf at the northern edge of Santa Monica.

Completed in 1893 and christened Port Los Angeles, the sinuous wharf provided the best shipping facility for the budding city. It also served as a mecca for fishermen, who found great sport along the wharf's walkway.

In 1897 Congress decided to create a harbor at San Pedro Bay, snuffing Southern Pacific's hopes for control of the Los Angeles shipping business. In 1916 Long Wharf was cut to half its length for use as a fishing pier, and in 1921 the remaining portion was removed entirely.

300 Bird's Eye View of Pleasure Pier, Santa Monica, Cal.

SANTA MONICA PIER

Entrance, Colorado and Ocean Avenues
Constructed 1907

In 1907 the Santa Monica Pier was built to carry the city's sewage out to sea. The adjoining Loof Pier was constructed in 1917 for more entertaining purposes—as a place for restaurants and amusements. It soon supported a roller coaster, a dance hall, and the still-standing carousel building, seen with an onion dome in the card above.

The gigantic La Monica Ballroom, with a dance floor large enough to accommodate five thousand twirling couples, opened in 1924 further out on the pier. The ballroom declined in the fifties, serving some time as a roller rink, and was finally torn down in 1963.

The merry-go-round is still spinning strong. It starred in *The Sting* in 1973, has just been exquisitely restored, and is open for riders every day until sundown at a mere quarter a whirl.

Bath House and Beach, Ocean Park, California.

THE OCEAN PARK BATHHOUSE

Ocean Park Beach
A. R. Fraser, architect, 1905. Destroyed by fire 1912

Before Abbot Kinney was hit by Italian fever, he developed Ocean Park, a southern suburb of Santa Monica. In less than five years Kinney and his partners turned a sandy wasteland into a small community humming with resort facilities and vacation housing, and in 1904 the town incorporated. Then Kinney moved on to devote all his energies to Venice.

When the bathhouse, built at a cost of $150,000,

445:—"Fare Please!" The Tram Between Santa Monica and Venice, Cal.

opened in 1905, a reporter described it as a "fairy palace." The enormous Turkish-style pavilion was surmounted by a skylight, which illuminated the heated plunge, and at night its needle-like towers were beaded with electric lights. That same year a forty-foot-wide boardwalk was constructed, connecting the extreme northern end of Ocean Park with Venice. It was later replaced by a cement walk and extended to Santa Monica. Trams like the one above made for pleasant travel along the strip.

Many of Ocean Park's buildings were destroyed by fire in 1912, and in 1924 another fire razed Lick Pier, Fraser Pier, and the Dome Theater.

VENICE OF AMERICA

Norman F. Marsh and C. H. Russell, architects; Abbot Kinney, founder. 1905

The development of Venice began in 1900, when Abbot Kinney, art connoisseur, tobacco mogul, and author of *Tasks by Twilight*, a book about "creative reproduction," commissioned Norman Marsh and C. H. Russell to bring a little bit of Italy to Los Angeles. Kinney envisioned his Venice as a western Chautauqua, where culture and education, in the form of lectures, plays, and concerts, would be accessible to the masses. He dredged sixteen miles of canals, a uniform four feet deep by forty feet wide, imported gondolas and gondoliers from Venice, and planted weeping willow and gum trees along the banks. He built a bathhouse large enough to accommodate five thousand bathers, constructed a square of buildings modeled on the Piazza San Marco, and hired a sixty-piece Italian orchestra to keep strollers in the mood. Visitors could rent or buy canal-side tents and cottages or could make day trips on the Pacific Railway.

796 – CANAL SCENE IN VENICE, CALIFORNIA.

797 – ARCADE, WINDWARD AVENUE, VENICE, CALIFORNIA.

High-minded entertainments soon gave way to more popular amusements when the Playa del Rey began to siphon off Venice's crowds. The Italian orchestra gave way to a ragtime band, Kinney erected a midway over his lagoon, and through the teens and early twenties Venice thrived as an amusement

798 – ON THE MIDWAY, VENICE, CALIFORNIA.

center, complete with a Ferris wheel, "shoot-the-chutes," and a miniature railway.

The rise of the automobile spelled doom for Kinney's dream; the narrow streets, ubiquitous canals, and complete lack of streets for through traffic repelled motorists, who turned elsewhere for fun. By 1930 all but three miles of the canals had been filled in to make roadways, and, while the amusement concessions remained, Venice was left with little charm.

Since then Venice has seen brief revivals—as a beatnik community in the fifties, as a home for the counterculture in the sixties, and today as a theater for roller skaters and body builders, who perform every weekend on Ocean Front Walk.

Warf Scene, Redondo, Cal. *pier from which the boat leaves.*

REDONDO BEACH

When Redondo Harbor lost in the competition to become Los Angeles's major commercial seaport, the area turned to the resort trade. As the terminus of three railroad lines, including the Pacific Electric, and as the home of an amusement park, the lavish Redondo Hotel, and a spectacular ten-acre carnation field, Redondo drew turn-of-the-century pleasure seekers by the thousands.

A throng of six thousand came to enjoy the bathhouse on its opening day—July 1, 1909—and all three plunges—one five feet deep, one nine feet deep, and one for chil-

2803 Bathing Pavilion and Street Scene, Redondo, California

dren—were packed by ten in the morning. In the afternoon the crowd was treated to a display of Japanese daytime fireworks, band concerts, and a diving contest. At dusk the building's exterior was illuminated by seven thousand electric lights, and the two three-tier fountains in the plunges glowed with colored lighting effects. One member of the crowd was so overcome by the sight that he seized an American flag and, waving it aloft, swam across the tank on his back, to the cheers of onlookers.

Redondo Beach lost much of its drawing power as an amusement area with the decline of the Pacific Electric, and the bathhouse was razed in 1943.

The Pike at Long Beach, Cal.

THE PIKE AT LONG BEACH

Originally on Seaside Boulevard from Pine Avenue to
Chestnut Place

This beachside stretch of amusements officially opened on

July 4, 1902, when the first Pacific Electric cars arrived
at Long Beach, bringing thousands to enjoy the palatial
new bathhouse—which offered both salt and freshwater
plunges, seven hundred private dressing rooms, and ten
bowling lanes—and to see the foundations laid for the

"Walk of a Thousand Lights." The Pike eventually boasted a 6,000-seat Assembly hall, a skating rink, funhouses, three ballrooms, and a roller coaster, much of which was scattered along the 1,800-foot Silvery Spray Pleasure Pier.

Most of the old Pike is gone today. Both pier and plunge have disappeared altogether, replaced by today's more mundane, family-oriented amusement zone.

San Pedro Harbor, California

SAN PEDRO HARBOR/LOS ANGELES HARBOR

From its early days as a crude, shallow harbor—known to sailors as "The Hell of California" because of the long hauls they had to make over mud flats and cliffs—Los Angeles Harbor has grown into the country's largest fishing and canning port.

In 1851 twenty-one-year-old Phineas Banning trudged ashore after a sea voyage from the East Coast, took a look at the three shacks that serviced the harbor, and decided that improvements were in order. Eleven years later he ran a warehouse, blacksmith shop, soap factory, and corrals in his new town of Wilmington, and managed a wharf and shipping channel.

When in the 1890s the city decided that it needed a major deep-water port, San Pedro Bay seemed the logical location—though not to the Southern Pacific Railroad, which lobbied greedily for Santa Monica as the site of the new port. The Army Board of Engineers decided in favor of San Pedro, work began in 1899, and by 1915, when the Panama Canal was opened, Los Angeles had a deep-water harbor.

Palace of the Doges Pavilion at Naples, Cal.

NAPLES

In 1905 A. M. Parsons dredged a portion of Los Alamitos Bay to form a small cove with an island in the center and began to advertise the subdivision as a paradise of "ornate and costly buildings, stairways, promenades, arches, boulevards, and water streets that are water streets. . . . No miasma, no mosquitos." He named the development Naples, although he built a duplicate of the Venetian Palace of the Doges at its entrance. A number of houses went up in 1906, as did Almira Hershey's Hotel Naples, a twin to her Hollywood Hotel.

The financial panic of 1907 forced Parsons to sell out, leaving Naples undeveloped until 1923, when new owners completed the bridges and canals.

The canal walls were severely damaged by the 1933 Long Beach earthquake, but were repaired, and Naples has thrived ever since.

C·65 CASINO WAY "ROMANCE PROMENADE", SHOWING YACHT CLUB AND NEW CASINO,

CATALINA ISLAND, CALIFORNIA

CATALINA ISLAND

Development of Catalina Island began during the last quarter of the nineteenth century, when William Banning formed the Santa Catalina Island Company for the purpose of turning the twenty-eight-mile-long island into a pleasure resort. Soon Catalina blossomed with elegant small hotels; an Island Villa, where tents could be rented for $1.50 a night; an aquarium; and a carrier-pigeon service that relayed the island's news to city newspapers in less than an hour.

William Wrigley, Jr., the chewing gum tycoon, bought

Island Villa, Catalina Island, Cal.

the island in 1919 and continued to develop its resort facilities. The circular Casino, designed by Weber and Spaulding and built on the northwest end of Crescent Bay in 1929, is legendary for its vast dance floor, floating on two inches of cork, inlaid with seven different hardwoods, and capable of accommodating 2,500 dancing couples.

Although Catalina is still a popular tourist spot, most of its interior remains undeveloped. The Santa Catalina Company acquired title to eighty-six percent of the island in 1975 and now administers the land jointly with the County of Los Angeles.

103

WALTER KNOTT
FOUNDER & OWNER OF
KNOTT'S BERRY-PLACE
Buena Park, California. 34.

KNOTT'S BERRY FARM

8039 Beach Boulevard
Founded by Walter and Cordelia Knott in 1934

Knott's Berry Farm, the oldest theme amusement park in the world, was born when Cordelia Knott introduced her sixty-five-cent chicken dinner to the buyers at her family's roadside berry stand in Buena Park. She sold eight dinners the first day, and soon word of Mrs. Knott's tasty cooking, as well as her husband's berries, brought the couple a thriving business. To keep customers happy while they waited in line, Walter Knott installed a few amusements, and today those occupy a 150-acre park bristling with rides and with replicas of sights of the Old West.

The chicken dinner business is now Mrs. Knott's Chicken Dinner Restaurant. The entire concern is still owned and operated by the Knott family.

DISNEYLAND

Between Harbor Boulevard and West Street
Walt Disney, chief designer. 1955

Ray Bradbury once suggested that Walt Disney be made mayor of Los Angeles. He considered Disney the only man in Los Angeles who could "get a working rapid transit system built without any more surveys, and turn it into a real attraction so that people will want to ride it."

He was referring, of course, to the slickly choreographed system of transportation that threads through Disneyland, the world-renowned seventy-six-acre Anaheim amusement kingdom. Almost every conceivable form of transportation—including rafts, steamships, bobsleds, canoes, a monorail, and a People Mover—whisk visitors through the park, which was built in 1955 on what had been a sweeping plain of orange trees.

Disney's dream city attracts hundreds of thousands of visitors every year to what looks like the world's largest movie set; the management suggests that visitors reserve at least eight hours to see the sights, which include a haunted mansion peopled with holographs, a fourteen-story replica of the Matterhorn, a seventy-two-horse carousel, a thrilling boat ride down a jungle river inhabited by mechanical hippos and crocodiles, and "It's a Small World," a lavish display of singing dolls first introduced at the 1964 New York World's Fair.

© Walt Disney Productions

105

Publishers and Dates of the Postcards

Page 2 Western Publishing & Novelty Co.; about 1928

13 M. Rieder; about 1906

14 Western Publishing & Novelty Co.; about 1940

15 Western Publishing & Novelty Co.; about 1940

16 Newman Post Card Co.; about 1910

17 Western Publishing & Novelty Co.; about 1930

18 Publisher unknown; 1910

19 Western Publishing & Novelty Co.; about 1935

20 M. Rieder; about 1904

21 Newman Post Card Co.; about 1904

23 Tichnor Art Company; about 1930

24 Western Publishing & Novelty Co.; about 1931

25 Western Publishing & Novelty Co.; about 1926

26 Van Ornum Colorprint Co.; about 1906

27 Western Publishing & Novelty Co.; about 1924

28 Newman Post Card Co.; about 1906

29 Clifton's/B. B. Thomas; about 1958

31 Geo. Rice and Sons; about 1906

32 Longshaw Card Co.; about 1932

33 Coca-Cola Bottling Company of Los Angeles; about 1976

34 Western Publishing & Novelty Co.; about 1924

35 Los Angeles Examiner; about 1912

36 Western Publishing & Novelty Co.; about 1928

37 Western Publishing & Novelty Co.; about 1924

39 Western Publishing & Novelty Co.; about 1970

40 M. Rieder; about 1908

41 M. Rieder; about 1908

42 Detroit Publishing Co.; about 1910

43 News Stand Distributors/ Tichnor Quality Views; about 1920

45 Mt. Lowe Post Card; about 1920

46 Pacific Novelty Company; about 1905

47 Mt. Lowe Post Card; about 1920

48 Newman Post Card Co.; about 1910

49 Newman Post Card Co.; about 1910

51 Western Publishing & Novelty Co.; about 1930

53 M. Kashower Co.; about 1925

54 Edward H. Mitchell; about 1906

55 Newman Post Card Co.; about 1916

56 Western Publishing & Novelty Co.; about 1930

57 Western Publishing & Novelty Co.; about 1930

58 E. C. Kropp Co.; about 1925

59 E. C. Kropp Co.; about 1926

Page 60   Newman Post Card Co.; about 1905

61   California Postcard Co.; about 1920

62   California Postcard Co.; about 1922

63   California Postcard Co.; about 1920

64   M. Kashower; about 1915

65   Western Publishing & Novelty Co.; about 1927

67   Mitock Publishers, Inc.; about 1978
Photograph by Craig Aurness

68   Western Publishing & Novelty Co.; about 1940

69   Western Publishing & Novelty Co.; about 1940

71   Western Publishing & Novelty Co.; about 1925

72   M. Kashower Co.; about 1930

73   Western Publishing & Novelty Co.; about 1940

74   Western Publishing & Novelty Co.; about 1955

75   Western Publishing & Novelty Co.; about 1940

76   Frashers Fotos; about 1940

77   Western Publishing & Novelty Co.; about 1940

79   Western Publishing & Novelty Co.; about 1930

80   Western Publishing & Novelty Co.; about 1935

81   Western Publishing & Novelty Co.; about 1915

83   M. Kashower Co.; about 1920

84   Western Publishing & Novelty Co.; about 1921

85   Robert Kashower; about 1935

87   M. Kashower Co.; about 1930

88   Oscar Newman; about 1906

89   M. Kashower Co.; about 1920

90   The Benham Co.; about 1906

91   M. Kashower Co.; about 1920

93   Edward H. Mitchell; about 1906

94   Edward H. Mitchell; about 1906

95   Edward H. Mitchell; about 1906

96   M. Rieder; about 1909

97   Cardinell-Vincent Co.; about 1909

98   Newman Post Card Co.; about 1908

99   M. Rieder; about 1910

100   M. Rieder; about 1915

101   Newman Post Card Co.; about 1906

102   Western Publishing & Novelty Co.; about 1935

103   Catalina Novelty Co.; about 1910

104   Publisher unknown; about 1940

105   Walt Disney Productions; about 1965

On Collecting Los Angeles Postcards

Old Los Angeles area postcards can be found with varying degrees of success at flea markets and antique stores, and through organizations of postcard collectors. Prices range from five cents to more than twenty dollars, depending on the age and rarity of the card and the conscience and savvy of the seller. Flea markets and the less polished antique stores are the most likely sources of bargains, once you know how to spot them.

Postcard collectors' clubs exist in many cities, and their meetings are the best places to find old postcards in quantity, including Los Angeles cards, and to get a sense of the range of prices and values. The Los Angeles area is fortunate to have several such clubs, and if you are interested in starting or adding to a postcard collection of your own, a visit to any of their meetings will prove a rewarding treat. The clubs, with the times and locations of their meetings, are as follows:

ANGELS FLIGHT POSTCARD CLUB: meets on the fourth Monday of each month, from 7:00 to 9:30 PM, at the California Federal Savings & Loan (in the rear of the building), 1900 West Sunset Boulevard (just east of Alvarado), Los Angeles.

CALIFORNIA ASSOCIATION OF POSTCARD COLLECTORS: meets on the second Saturday of each month, from 7:30 to 10:00 PM, at the Mercury Savings & Loan, in the Mercury Room (accessible from the security lot at the end of the drive on the east side of the building), 7612 Edinger, Westminster.

PASADENA POSTCARD CLUB: meets on the second Tuesday of each month, from 7:30 to 9:30 PM, at the First Methodist Church, Colorado Boulevard, Pasadena. (Enter by way of Los Robles Avenue; take Converse Alley, which is halfway between Colorado and Green Streets; go east to the church parking lot, then turn right to the door closest to Green Street.)

SAN DIEGO POSTCARD CLUB: meets on the third Tuesday of each month, from 7:00 to 9:00 PM, at the San Diego Facility Building, in "Training Room" 15, 555 Overland Avenue (off Clairmont Mesa Boulevard between Highway 163 and I-15), San Diego.

SANTA MONICA POSTCARD CLUB: meets on the first Thursday of each month, from 6:00 to 9:00 PM, at the Fairview Branch Library, in the Community Room (on the east side of the library, with a separate entrance front and rear), 2101 Ocean Park Boulevard, Santa Monica.

Postcard clubs also exist throughout the rest of the

country. To find out if there is one in your area, send a stamped, self-addressed envelope with your inquiry to: Post Card Club Federation, John H. McClinton, Director, Box 27, Somerdale, New Jersey 08083.

Generally speaking, the older Los Angeles cards are more valuable than the newer ones, many of which are still made and can be found on racks in card shops and newsstands throughout the area. Common cards of major sights dating from the 1910-era postcard boom through the linen era of the 1940s range in price from ten cents to two dollars. Higher prices are charged for pre-1902 postcards, cards of hard-to-find sights, buildings never built, or images made from plans that changed before construction. Because Los Angeles has grown so rapidly, and changed its image for tourists so drastically through the years, old cards of some tourist attractions are surprisingly rare—of the Hollywood Sign for example—because popular interest has only developed quite recently. Hunting for rarities can be fun, because when you finally find that unusual postcard the asking price is generally reasonable. The most expensive cards of all are the old novelty cards—from special sets with fancy decorative borders, mechanical cards with pieces that move, hold-to-light cards with tiny built-in windows, and other unusual limited edition creations.

One further twist to postcard collecting is that the presence of such objects as early trucks, airplanes, or zeppelins on cards can increase their value dramatically, sometimes to the dismay of the Los Angeles postcard collector who may only be interested in the building over which the zeppelin is passing.

If you are interested in reading more about postcard collecting or the history of postcards, the most complete book on the subject is *Picture Postcards in the United States, 1893—1918* by George and Dorothy Miller (New York: Clarkson N. Potter, 1976). Another useful guide for the beginning collector is *The Book of Postcard Collecting* by Thomas E. Range (New York: E. P. Dutton, 1980). The Gotham Book Mart stocks all available books and journals about postcards, and sells them through the mail. Visit in person if you are ever in New York City, or write for a catalogue at 41 West 47th Street, New York, NY 10036.

Index to the Sights

A & M Records   63

Al Malaikah Temple   36

Alexandria Hotel   28

Angel's Flight   20, 21

Angelus Temple   52, 53

Automobile Club of Southern California   34

Beverly Hills Electric Fountain   80

Beverly Hills Hotel   81

Biltmore Hotel   27

Bradbury Building   30, 31

Brown Derby   59

Bullock's Wilshire   57

Busch Gardens   41

Capitol Records Tower   74

Carthay Circle Theater   78, 79

Catalina Island   102, 103

Cawston Ostrich Farm   42

Chaplin Studio   63

Christie Studios   61

Christmas Tree Lane   43

Church of Our Lady Queen of the Angels   12, 13

City Hall   17

Clifton's Pacific South Seas Cafeteria   29

Coca-Cola Bottling Company Building   33

Coogan, Jackie, Home of   84

Crossroads of the World   76

Davies, Marion, Home of   86, 87

Disneyland   105

Eastern Columbia Building   32

Echo Park   54

Edison Building   24

Examiner Building   35

Farmers Market   77

Forest Lawn Memorial Park   50, 51

Grauman's Chinese Theatre   72, 73

Grauman's Egyptian Theatre   70, 71

Herald Examiner Building   35

Hollywood   60

Hollywood Bowl   68, 69

Hollywood Hotel   64

Hollywood Sign   66, 67

Hollywoodland   65

Knott's Berry Farm   104

Long Beach   98, 99

Long Wharf at Santa Monica   88

Los Angeles County Courthouse   16

Los Angeles Harbor   100

Los Angeles Memorial Coliseum   37

Los Angeles Public Library   25

Los Angeles Times Building, first   18

Los Angeles Times Building, present   19

MacArthur Park   55

Mann's Chinese Theatre   72, 73

Mount Lowe   44–47

Naples   101

NBC Radio City   75

Ocean Park Bathhouse   90, 91

Old Plaza Church   12, 13

One Bunker Hill Building   24

Pasadena Tournament of Roses Parade   40

Philharmonic Auditorium   26

Pickfair   82, 83

Redondo Beach   96, 97

Richfield Building   22, 23

San Fernando Mission   48

San Pedro Harbor   100

Santa Monica Pier   89

Set for *Robin Hood*   62

Shrine Auditorium   36

Temple, Shirley, Home of   85

Towers of Simon Rodia   38, 39

Southern Pacific Depot at San Fernando   49

Temple Baptist Church   26

Union Passenger Station   14, 15

Van de Kamp's Holland Dutch Bakers   58

Venice of America   93–95

Watts Towers   38, 39

Westlake Park   55

Wilshire Boulevard   56

Acknowledgments

The following people very kindly loaned postcards from their private collections for inclusion in this book. The author extends thanks to them for their generous help:

Andreas Brown and the Gotham Book Mart (whose cards appear on pp. 13, 18, 35, 40, 42, 47, 49, 51, 60, 84, 91, 94, 96, 97, 98, and 103)

Glen Dawson (whose cards appear on pp. 31, 46, and 48)

Norm Fogel (whose cards appear on pp. 29 and 79)

Christy Johnson (whose card appears on p. 76)

Ruthann Lehrer (whose card appears on p. 32)

Paul Kreyling (whose cards appear on pp. 59 and 64)

Gary Wright (whose card appears on p. 85)

For help in researching the cards and the text, thanks to Joel Berger and Nat Sherman of the Western Publishing & Novelty Company, Lee Brown and members of the Santa Monica Post Card Club, Caryn Diamond, Mary Dill, Bill Luckey, Carol Nevitt, Paul Nevitt, John Neyenesch, George Purcell, the California Room at the Los Angeles Public Library, the Boston Public Library, and the New York Public Library.

Special thanks to Polly Cone, Eric Kampmann, Ellen Morgan, and Ken Boege.